Geo. H. Moore

Engraved by A. B. Hall, for

The Historical Magazine

George Henry Moore, LL. D.

A MEMOIR.

By Rev. HOWARD CROSBY. D. D.

MORRISANIA, N. Y.

1870.

The following Memoir, prepared for THE HISTORICAL MAGAZINE and originally published in that work, has been re-produced in this form, in an edition of thirty copies, exclusively for private circulation among the personal friends of Mr. Moore.

MORRISANIA, N. Y., 1870. H. B. D.

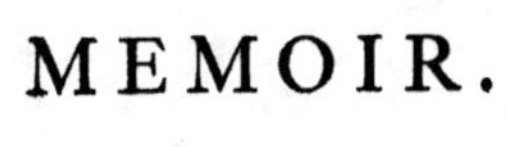

MEMOIR.

MEMORIAL.

Men of worth shrink from notoriety. They live for their work; not for themselves. Their ambition is to do; not to appear. Idlers and adventurers will climb up dizzy heights, to carve their names in the rock; but the true man cuts down the forest, builds the house, and tills the soil, leaving something better than an empty name for the generations to come. The heroes of the world have never been mustered by History; it is only the Divine roll-call, at the great consummation, that can select those modest souls. Where one great man escapes into fame, a hundred enclose themselves in their cocoons of industry, fond of concealment and all unconscious of their coming colors. If one wishes to see the good, the useful, and the true, among men, he must look beneath the surface, or he will make a defective estimate. Some good grows up into visibility; but a vast amount lies as gold in the mine; and when the wealth of virtue that the world possesses, is to be reckoned, the jewels that hide from the public gaze are to be remembered as forming the largest portion of the whole amount.

It is a very refreshing experience to the

healthy mind to turn from the crowded highway, where merit is disfigured with dust and tinsel, and clamorous applause marks alike the good and evil, and find, in calmer scenes, the contented spirit, a reward to itself, achieving its progress, not by the guidance of popular impulse, but by the inward promptings of the truth. It is principally through such laborers that the world moves; and it is around such that true happiness gathers.

For many years, it has been our good fortune to watch the busy life of a toiler of this sort; and, if we regarded only his personal peace, we should not now mention his name; but, for the encouragement of others and a protest against the noise, and bluster, and sensation of the day, we must wound his feelings for this once.

George Henry Moore was born in Concord, New Hampshire, on the twentieth of April, 1823.

His father was well known in his native State, for his high political and literary abilities; and, toward the close of his life, filled the onerous and responsible position of Postmaster at San Francisco, where he lent his energies to the growth of that Pacific metropolis. Mr. Moore's uncle, Governor Isaac Hill, had a national fame.

George, the oldest of four sons, came to New York, in 1839, at the age of sixteen;

and, by a course of resolute self-denial, made an honorable way for himself and his three brothers, through a collegiate education, at the New York University, his youngest brother being graduated from that institution in 1851. George himself was graduated in 1843. His fellow-students of that day love to testify to his untiring perseverance and genial disposition, throughout his college course, in which he mingled the devotion of the scholar with the instincts of generous friendship.

In 1841, while a Sophomore in College, he entered the service of the New York Historical Society, as Assistant Librarian, George Folsom being the Librarian.

The Historical Society, at that time, was a quiet potentiality, a respectable egg, over which the influences of Washington Irving, George Bancroft, and other such were brooding with faint hopes of a hatch. It was stowed away in a corner of the University Building; and led a very dingy life. From the start, Mr. Moore, as Assistant Librarian, became the chief workman in the concern,—George Folsom, and afterwards, George Gibbs, and then Mr. Moore's venerable father, who were Librarians, wisely acting as figure-heads to the office; and allowing the genius and industry of the Assistant to be untrammelled. A new life entered the old bones. Growth, order, thrift, were the magical results of young Moore's energy. In 1849, the Historical Society did not know itself. It had become a power in the community. The best men of the City thronged its *séances*, (where portly Janitor Smith dealt out the chocolate); papers of highest interest were read in its rooms; its patronage was sought by the historical explorers of the land; and rich men were honored by contributing to its resources. While all this was done, the cunning workman who had wrought the change remained in obscurity as the Assistant Librarian.

When Mr. Moore's father resigned his post as Librarian, Doctor Edward Robinson, who always had an eye to the fitness of things, proposed the son as the rightful successor.

From that day to this, a period of twenty years, Mr. Moore, if we may be classical and not jocose, has been the Atlas of the Historical Society. To change the figure and conform the better to modern science, Mr. Moore has been the central Sun of the Historical Society's system, around which President, Vice-president, and all the other officers and members, have most becomingly pursued their orbits. Whenever any one thinks of the Historical Society, George H. Moore appears at once to his imagination. He *is* the Historical Society, in its walking, talking avatar. While the Society has taken the first rank among kindred institutions in this country, and appropriately moved itself out of the University garret into a neat and beautiful house of its own, it would foil a cynic to seek the first error of management in design or execution on the part of the ruling spirit of the noble enterprise.

In that fine edifice, on Second Avenue, within the classic purlieu of St. Mark's, is gathered the richest material for our country's history; while Nineveh and Egypt are represented to the undoubted satisfaction of the bust of Herodotus, over the main door. No visitor in New York is guiltless who has failed to enter this shrine of Clio and lulled his spirit in its quiet, historic atmosphere. No man can say that he knows the institutions of New York, if he does not know GEORGE H. MOORE. The hearty welcome, the kindliness of soul, overflowing in voice and manner, the genial greeting of eye and hand, which Clio's high-priest accords to devout worshippers, are worth a long journey of themselves.

Off the main Library hall is Mr. Moore's laboratory. Here, his untiring industry has accomplished its successes. When he had completed the years of detail that were necessary to syst matize the literary property of the Society and had reduced a very dismal chaos to cosmical order, he turned his attention to utilizing his large information and mature judgment, for the benefit of the historic world.

In 1860, Mr. Moore published an octavo of

one hundred and fifteen pages, on the *Treason of Charles Lee*,* a work which excited deserved interest and showed the accurate analysis and scholarly abilities of its author. In 1862, he published his *Historical Notes on the employment of Negroes in the American Army of the Revolution*,† a most opportune and influential publication, when the negro-soldier-question was pressing itself on the Nation, in the fearful scenes of civil strife; and, in 1866, he *aroused* (rather than *excited*) public attention by his *Notes on the History of Slavery in Massachusetts*,‡ an octavo of two hundred and fifty-six pages. This work fairly startled the Pharisees, who had smoothed their paunches with a comfortable feeling of their own immaculateness, and put a valuable foot-note to some loose pages of history.

---

* "*Mr. Lee's Plan—March* 29, 1777." | *The* | *Treason of Charles Lee* | *Major General* | *second in command in the American Army* | *of the Revolution.* | By George H. Moore, | Librarian of the New York Historical Society. | [Read before the Society, on Tuesday evening, June 22, 1858.] | "*The evil that men do lives after them.*" | New Xork: | Charles Scribner, 124 Grand Street. | M.DCCC.LX |
Octavo pp. xii, 115. Portraits and fac-similes.

† *Historical Notes* | *on the* | *Employment of Negroes* | *in the* | *American Army of the Revolution.* | By | George H. Moore, | Librarian of the New York Historical Society. | New York: | Charles T. Evans, 532 Broadway. | 1862.
Octavo, pp. 24.

‡ *Notes* | *on the* | *History of Slavery* | *in* | *Massachusetts* | By George H. Moore | Librarian of the New York Historical Society and Corresponding | Member of the Massachusetts Historical Society. | Quis nescit, primam esse historiæ legem, ne quid falsi | dicere audeat? deinde ne quid falsi | dicere audeat? deinde ne quid veri non audeat? | —*Cic. de Orat.*, II., 15. | New York: | D. Appleton & Co. 443 & 445 Broadway | M.DCCC.LXVI. |
Octavo, pp. iv, 256.

This was followed by a tract, entitled *Additional Notes on Slavery in Massachusetts*,* a clincher to the former. Mr. Moore has also been a frequent contributor to *The Evening Post*, *Commercial Advertiser*, *Journal of Commerce*, and the HISTORICAL MAGAZINE, where his signature of E. Y. E. is widely-known throughout the historical world.

A more valuable work than these, and one on which Mr. Moore's fame will chiefly rest, as an accurate, laborious, and scholarly writer and historian, is the *History of the Jurisprudence of New York*, still incomplete and unpublished; but which is, and has been, for a long time, engaging his faithful energies.

In 1860, Mr. Moore was called to the Chair of Legal History, in the New York University; but he declined this fitting tribute to his worth. From the same institution, he subsequently received the degree of LL.D.

We wish that we felt at liberty to introduce our readers within the sacred circle of Mr. Moore's home. Of course we cannot. We can only say that the home is all that could be expected from such a man. Mr. Moore was married, on the twenty-first of October, 1850; and with a wife who appreciates him and children of peculiar promise, his lot is to be envied, furnish-

---

* *Additional Notes | on the | History of Slavery in Massachusetts, | G. H. M. |*
Small quarto, pp. 15.

ing a fair model of the unostentatious, literary, useful, upright, and contented life—the life to which "*fides et ingeni benigna vena*" are of higher value than the "*ebur*" and "*aureum*" and "*trabes Hymettiae.*"

New York City. H. C.

www.ingramcontent.com/pod-product-compliance
Lightning Source LLC
LaVergne TN
LVHW011143110826
845150LV00008B/2492

* 9 7 8 1 4 1 8 1 9 2 9 5 2 *